Flavou...
KE...

RECIPES

G000277619

Compiled by Julia Skinner

THE FRANCIS FRITH COLLECTION

www.francisfrith.com

First published in the United Kingdom in 2011 by The Francis Frith Collection®

This edition published exclusively for Bradwell Books in 2012
For trade enquiries see: www.bradwellbooks.com or tel: 0800 834 920
ISBN 978-1-84589-564-8

British Library Cataloguing in Publication Data

Flavours of ... Kent - Recipes
Compiled by Julia Skinner

The Francis Frith Collection
Oakley Business Park,
Wylye Road, Dinton,
Wiltshire SP3 5EU
Tel: +44 (0) 1722 716 376
Email: info@francisfrith.co.uk
www.francisfrith.com

Printed and bound in Malaysia
Contains material sourced from responsibly managed forests

Front Cover: **FOLKESTONE, A COCKLES AND WHELKS STALL c1965** F35154p
Frontispiece: **SHALMSFORD STREET, 1906** 53465

The colour-tinting is for illustrative purposes only, and is not intended to be historically accurate

AS WITH ANY HISTORICAL DATABASE, THE FRANCIS FRITH ARCHIVE IS CONSTANTLY BEING
CORRECTED AND IMPROVED, AND THE PUBLISHERS WOULD WELCOME INFORMATION ON
OMISSIONS OR INACCURACIES

CONTENTS

RECIPE

WATERCRESS SOUP

Watercress has been eaten in Britain for centuries, but in earlier times it was mainly valued for its medicinal, anti-scorbutic properties. It was only adopted into the general diet in the early 19th century, when it began to be commercially and hygienically cultivated in large quantities. The first watercress farm in Britain was opened by Will Springhead in Kent in 1808, at Northfleet, near Gravesend, and watercress is still produced commercially in the county. Traditionally-grown watercress is cultivated in flowing watercourses of mineral-rich water of the highest purity, making this a super-food packed with nutrients, with a distinctive peppery, slightly bitter, flavour.

> 50g/2oz butter
> 2 bunches of watercress with their stalks removed,
>   washed and chopped
> 1 medium onion, chopped
> 25g/1oz plain flour
> 600ml/1 pint milk
> 450ml/ ¾ pint chicken or vegetable stock
> 6 tablespoonfuls single cream

Melt the butter in a large pan, and gently fry the watercress and onion for a few minutes until softened. Stir in the flour and cook for a further one minute. Slowly stir in the milk, a little at a time, and then the stock. Bring to the boil, stirring all the time, until thickened, then cover and simmer gently for 30 minutes. Remove from the heat and cool for a few minutes, then liquidize. Before serving, add the cream and reheat gently, taking care not to allow the soup to boil. Serve with a swirl of cream and a sprig of watercress leaves to garnish.

GRAVESEND, THE CLOCK TOWER 1902 49026

3

RAMSGATE, HARBOUR PARADE AND NEW ROAD c1920 68467

Kent's long coastline made fishing an important part of life in the county in the past. For centuries the coastal towns of the Isle of Thanet had a strong seafaring and fishing tradition, and in the 1880s Ramsgate had the largest fishing fleet in south-east England – 144 vessels all told. Although the fishing industry has declined dramatically in recent years, there are still around 130 licensed vessels operating from the Kent coast. Kent's main fishing ports are Whitstable, Ramsgate and Folkestone, but small boats also operate from the beaches at Deal, Hythe and Dungeness.

RECIPE

TWICE LAID FISHCAKES

This recipe for fishcakes is so named because it includes chopped hard boiled eggs. It would originally have been made with cod, but an alternative firm-fleshed white fish such as haddock, whiting, pollack or coley can be used instead. It can also be made with cooked white fish and mashed potatoes leftover from a previous meal.

350g/12oz white fish fillets, with the skin removed
300ml/ ½ pint milk
350g/12oz cooked mashed potatoes
2 eggs, hard boiled and shelled
1 extra egg, for dipping
175g/6oz fresh wholemeal breadcrumbs
A pinch of freshly ground black pepper

Pre-heat the oven to 190°C/375°/Gas Mark 5 and grease a baking sheet. Put the milk in a large pan and slide in the fish fillets. Bring slowly to the boil, then reduce the heat to simmer and cook the fish very gently for 3-5 minutes, until the flesh is just tender. Remove the fish from the pan and drain well, and reserve the milk for later. Carefully remove and discard any bones from the fish. Use a fork to flake the fish into a bowl, then add the mashed potatoes and mix well together, adding a little of the reserved milk to the mixture to help it bind together. Chop the hard boiled eggs into small pieces, then gently stir them into the fish mixture. Add pepper to taste. Divide the mixture into balls and dip them into the beaten egg, then roll them in the breadcrumbs to coat them on all sides. Place the balls on the baking sheet and bake in the pre-heated oven for about 15-20 minutes until they are crisp and golden. Alternatively, they can be deep fried in hot fat or oil if preferred.

BROADSTAIRS, THE HARBOUR 1897 39592

Broadstairs grew into one of Kent's most popular seaside towns in the 19th century, but before that it was a small fishing village known as 'Bradstow' whose fishermen ventured as far as the waters off Iceland to fish for cod. At the time of the above photograph, cod would have been a commonplace catch for Kent's fishermen, but this is now becoming a rare and expensive fish. Today's fishermen mainly operate from small day boats fishing the English Channel. Their most valuable catches are various varieties of sole, sea bass, cod and lobster, but they also bring in many delicious and cheaper alternatives to cod, such as pollack and gurnard (a bizarre-looking fish with excellent flesh), as well as large quantities of whelks.

RECIPE

SEA BASS BAKED WITH HONEY AND ONIONS

Sea bass is one of the finest of fish, with a wonderful flavour and an excellent texture. It is at its best when lightly stuffed and quickly grilled or oven baked, so that its delicious skin becomes crisp and aromatic, while the flesh remains tender and succulent. This recipe gives the quantities for a special dinner for two, with one whole fish per person – increase the quantities to feed more.

2 whole sea bass, cleaned, boned and gutted
1 large onion, finely chopped
2 cloves of garlic, crushed or finely chopped
2 tablespoonfuls olive oil
4-5 sprigs fresh thyme
2 tablespoonfuls runny honey
Salt and freshly ground black pepper
Olive oil, for drizzling

Pre-heat the oven to 200°C/400°C/Gas Mark 6. Use a sharp knife to score the skin across the fish with about 5 shallow diagonal cuts. Heat the oil in a frying pan and gently sauté the onion and garlic for about 5-8 minutes, until soft. Take the pan off the heat. Strip the thyme leaves off the stem and add to the onion and garlic. Mix together, season to taste, then leave to cool a little. Smear the honey on both sides of the cavity of each fish, then fill the cavity with the onion and thyme mixture, reserving any that is left over. Use kitchen string to tie up the fish, to secure it during cooking. Lay the fish in a baking tray or ovenproof dish, and add any leftover onion and thyme mixture. Sprinkle some salt and pepper over the fish and drizzle them with olive oil. Bake towards the top of the pre-heated oven – uncovered – for about 20-25 minutes. Test to see whether the fish is cooked by poking it with a sharp-pointed knife to see if the flesh at the centre is opaque – but do not overcook. Remove the string and serve immediately, with any cooking juices from the pan poured over the fish.

DOVER, THE PROMENADE 1924 76042

RECIPE

DOVER SOLE WITH FRESH HERBS

Although the delicious fish called the Dover sole is famously named after Dover on the Kent coast, it is not exclusively found there. This fish is caught in the seas from Norway to the Mediterranean, but probably got its name because Dover was the port where it was landed in quantity and from where it was transported to the London markets. One of the most expensive of white fish, Dover sole is best cooked very simply so that its fine, delicate flavour can be enjoyed. Serves 4.

> 4 Dover sole, with the fins and dark skin removed
> (the white skin should be left on, and can be eaten)
> 2-3 tablespoonfuls of seasoned plain flour
> 3 tablespoonfuls of olive oil
> 25g/1oz unsalted butter
> Juice of 1 lemon
> 1 tablespoonful of chopped fresh herbs such as tarragon,
>   dill, parsley

Coat both sides of the fish in the seasoned flour. Heat the oil in a large, wide, non-stick frying pan. Cook the fish one or two at a time over a medium heat for a few minutes on each side, until they are golden brown and cooked through, then keep them warm whilst the others are cooking. Add the butter to the remaining oil in the pan and heat until it has melted. Stir in the lemon juice and the chopped fresh herbs and mix it all together. Pour the buttery sauce over the fish and serve immediately.

RECIPE

ANGELS ON HORSEBACK

Whitstable on the Kent coast is famous for its oysters, and holds an oyster festival in late July each year. Whitstable had a fleet of over 100 oyster yawls in the 19th century; the last remaining yawl in the town, 'Favourite', built in 1891, is displayed on the beachside near the Royal Native Oyster Stores. Native oysters have a fuller, more intense flavour than imported varieties. The old 'R in the month' method of telling when they are best to eat still holds good, so look for them from September to April. A dish enjoyed locally is the Whitstable Dredgerman's Breakfast – streaky bacon fried until the fat runs, then covered with shelled oysters and cooked for a few more minutes, served with thick slices of bread and butter and a mug of strong tea. This recipe for oysters was a popular snack in Victorian times and it still makes a delicious snack or appetizer for modern tastes.

> 16 oysters, removed from their shells
> Fresh lemon juice
> 8 rashers of streaky bacon with their rinds removed
> 8 small slices of bread
> Butter
> Paprika, or a dash of Tabasco sauce (optional)

Pre-heat the oven to 200°C/400°C/Gas Mark 6.

Sprinkle each oyster with a little lemon juice. Lay the bacon rashers on a board, slide the back of a knife along each one to stretch it and then cut it in half crosswise. Wrap a piece of bacon around each oyster and secure with a wooden cocktail stick. Arrange the bacon-wrapped oysters on a baking sheet. Put the oysters and bacon into the pre-heated hot oven and cook for 8-10 minutes. Whilst the bacon and oysters are cooking, toast the bread. When the bacon is cooked through, spread each slice of hot toast with butter, and place a bacon-wrapped oyster on top of each piece. Sprinkle with a little paprika or a dash of Tabasco sauce, if used, before serving.

Both brown and red shrimps are found in abundance around the Kent coast. On the left of this photograph below of the village of Pegwell Bay are the Floral Tea Gardens, followed by the Pear Tree Inn, which later became Samuel Banger's potted shrimp paste factory. His small paste pots had highly decorated lids depicting scenes of Pegwell; today they are valuable and sought-after antiques.

PEGWELL, THE VILLAGE 1907 58296

The Romney Marsh is a region of flat wetland reclaimed from the sea that encompasses an area near the coast over west Kent and East Sussex. A specific breed of sheep developed there, the Romney Marsh, which is large, big boned and sturdy, able to feed and thrive in wet situations and robust enough to withstand the winds that sweep across the grazing grounds from the English Channel. Feeding on the rich pastures of these low-lying windswept salt marshes gives a distinctive flavour to the good quality meat of the Romney Marsh sheep and lambs that graze there. For many centuries Ashford has been one of the main market centres for the Romney Marsh; it still has a busy livestock market, with buyers from all over England attending the Autumn Sheep Sales.

ASHFORD, HIGH STREET 1906 53444

RECIPE

LAMB AND BARLEY CASSEROLE

Use well-flavoured Kentish lamb to make this tasty casserole. Pearl barley is a bulking ingredient that was often used in lamb stews or soups in traditional British cookery, to make the meat go further.

1.4kg/3 lb lean boneless leg or shoulder of lamb, trimmed of fat
   and cut into 4cm (1½ inch) cubes
2 tablespoonfuls plain flour
Salt and pepper
3 rashers of streaky bacon, de-rinded & chopped into small pieces
25g/1oz butter
2 onions, finely chopped
2 carrots, sliced
115g/4oz turnip or swede, peeled and diced
2 celery sticks, cut into small slices
50g/2oz pearl barley
2 teaspoonfuls of finely chopped mixed fresh herbs: thyme,
   rosemary, parsley
300ml/ ½ pint lamb or beef stock
A little extra finely chopped fresh parsley, to garnish

Pre-heat the oven to 150°C/300°/Gas Mark 3. Put the flour in a bowl and season it with salt and pepper. Toss the lamb cubes in the seasoned flour so that all sides are coated. Dry fry the bacon pieces in a large frying pan until the fat has run, then take them out of the pan and put into a large ovenproof casserole. Melt the butter in the pan, then add the lamb cubes, a few at a time, and sauté them for about 2 minutes, to seal the meat on all sides, but do not allow it to colour. Remove the meat from the pan and put in the casserole. Fry the onions, carrots, celery and swede or turnip in the remaining fat in the pan for 5-10 minutes until lightly browned, then add them to the casserole. Add the pearl barley and herbs to the casserole, then pour in the stock. Give it all a good stir, then cover the casserole dish with its lid and cook in the pre-heated oven for 2-2½ hours, until the lamb is tender. Serve hot, sprinkled with finely chopped fresh parsley.

'GOD SEND THEE A YOWLING CROP...'

Apples are an important crop in Kent, so it is not surprising that fine cider is made in the county. In most cider-making counties of England in the past, a traditional ceremony was held every year which was known as 'wassailing' (from the Anglo-Saxon words 'Waes Hal', meaning 'good health'). Wassailing took place in the winter around Christmas time and the New Year, usually on Twelfth Night (January 5th); jugs of cider were carried into the orchards, most of which would be drunk, and the rest would be poured around the roots of the apple trees. A lot of noise would be made with banging of pots and pans, to drive away evil spirits from the trees, and wake up the trees for the spring; sometimes shotguns would be fired through the branches. Special cakes would often be eaten, pieces of cake or bread, soaked in cider, would be placed in the trees as a thanksgiving to the tree spirit and to ensure a good crop in the following year, and a traditional wassailing song would be sung. The first recorded account of wassailing in England occurred at Fordwich in Kent (near Canterbury) in 1585, when it was written that groups of young men went between the orchards performing the rite in return for a reward of food, ale or money. Wassailing was also called 'howling' or 'yowling' in Kent, and a Kentish wassailing song was included by Thomas George Crippen in his book 'Christmas and Christmas Lore', published in 1923:

> *'Stand fast twig, bear well top,*
> *God send thee a yowling crop,*
> *Every twig, apples big,*
> *Every bough, apples enow.*
> *Hats full! Caps full!*
> *Half bushel bags full!*
> *And my pockets full too! Huzzah!'*

RECIPE

PORK WITH APPLES AND CIDER SAUCE

Use Kentish cider to make a delicious creamy sauce to accompany pork in this recipe.

25g/1oz butter
500g/1¼ lbs pork tenderloin, cut into small pieces
12 baby onions or shallots, peeled and left whole
2 teaspoonfuls grated lemon rind
300ml/ ½ pint dry Kentish cider
150ml/ ¼ pint stock
2 crisp eating apples, cored and sliced but not peeled
3 tablespoonfuls chopped fresh parsley
100ml/4 fl oz whipping cream
Salt and pepper

Heat the butter in a large frying pan, and brown the pork in batches. Transfer the pork to a bowl. Add the onions to the pan and cook gently until they are soft. Stir in the lemon rind, cider and stock, increase heat and boil for a few minutes. Return the pork to the pan, reduce heat and cook gently for 25-30 minutes, until the meat is tender. Add the apples to the pan and cook for a further 5 minutes.

Use a slotted spoon to transfer the pork, apples and onions to a warmed serving dish, and keep warm. Stir the cream and parsley into the liquid remaining in the cooking pan, and allow the sauce to bubble so that it thickens slightly. Season to taste, then pour over the pork and serve whilst it is hot.

There has been a settlement at Faversham since Roman times; this little town at the head of a tidal creek had a small medieval port and still has a commercial quay. The Guildhall in Faversham was originally built in 1574 as a market hall; it was rebuilt in 1814, except for the splendid timber arches on which it rests, and the open-sided ground floor served as a shelter for market-stall-holders and their customers. Faversham is the home of Britain's oldest brewer still in business – the Shepherd Neame brewery, producer of such traditional cask ales as Canterbury Jack, Spitfire Premium Kentish Ale and Bishop's Finger Kentish Strong Ale.

FAVERSHAM, THE GUILDHALL c1960 F13079

RECIPE

BEEF BRAISED IN BEER

Use your own favourite Kentish beer or ale to make this traditional recipe from the county for a beef stew.

1kg/2 lbs chuck or stewing steak
50g/2oz plain flour
Salt and pepper
3 tablespoonfuls of cooking oil
2 carrots, cut into thin slices
50g/2oz mushrooms, cut into slices
2 onions, peeled and finely sliced
2 sticks of celery, cut into thin slices
1 tablespoonful tomato purée (tomato paste)
300ml/ ½ pint beef stock
300ml/ ½ pint beer or ale
1 bay leaf

Trim any fat off the meat, then cut it into neat 4cm (1½ inch) cubes. Put the flour in a bowl and season it with salt and pepper. Toss the cubes of meat in the seasoned flour so that all sides are coated. Heat 2 tablespoonfuls of the cooking oil in a large, shallow pan, then cook the cubes of meat in batches until they are lightly browned on all sides. Remove the meat from the pan and put it into a large ovenproof casserole. Add the final tablespoonful of oil to the pan, then cook the sliced onions until soft and well browned, adding the remaining vegetables towards the end. Add the vegetables to the casserole dish. Mix the beef stock with the beer and pour it over the meat and vegetables, and add the bay leaf. Bake in the pre-heated oven for 2-2½ hours, until the meat is tender. If the gravy needs further thickening before serving, mix one tablespoonful of cornflour with one tablespoonful of the gravy, stir it into the casserole and cook for a further 10 minutes. Remove the bay leaf before serving.

RECIPE

KENTISH CHICKEN PUDDING

This traditional Kentish recipe for a chicken pudding reflects the time in the past when many housewives only had a fire with a cauldron hanging over it on which to cook the family's meals. The pudding would have been wrapped up in a pudding cloth that had been liberally sprinkled with flour to make it waterproof, and then boiled in the cauldron along with the vegetables to accompany it, which would have been cooked separately in nets – an early version of a 'boil-in-the-bag' meal!

If you don't want to bother with cutting the meat off a whole chicken (or chicken joints) for this recipe, you can use chicken breast instead, cut into small cubes.

For the filling:
1 chicken, weighing about 1.6kg/3½ lbs
   (or the equivalent in chicken joints,
   or 450g/1 lb chicken breast)
115g/4oz button mushrooms
2 thick slices of cooked ham
1 tablespoonful chopped fresh parsley
25g/1oz plain flour, seasoned with salt and pepper
1 onion, peeled and chopped
Salt and pepper
300ml/ ½ pint chicken stock

For the suet crust pastry:
225g/8oz self-raising flour
115g/4oz shredded suet
Salt and pepper
Water to mix

Joint the chicken with a sharp knife, take the meat off the bone and cut it into small pieces. Toss the chicken pieces in seasoned flour so that all sides are coated. Coarsely chop the mushrooms, ham, and parsley and mix with the chopped onion.

Make the suet crust pastry by mixing together the self-raising flour, suet, salt and pepper in a bowl, adding enough water to form a smooth, but not sticky, dough. Take two-thirds of the dough and roll it out on a lightly floured surface and use it to line a greased 1.2 litre (2 pint) pudding basin. Fill the lined pudding basin with layers of chicken pieces and the chopped ham, mushroom, parsley and onion mixture, seasoning each layer to taste, then pour in the stock. Brush the top edge of the crust with water, roll out the remaining pastry to make a lid, and place it on top of the mixture. Press the pastry edges well together to seal them, and trim.

Cover the top of the pudding basin with a lid made from a pleated piece of greaseproof paper (to allow room for the pudding to expand and rise during cooking), followed by a piece of pleated foil, firmly tied on with string. Place the basin in a large saucepan of boiling water, cover the pan with its lid, and steam over boiling water for 3 hours. Top up the pan with more boiling water from time to time, and be sure not to let the pan boil dry.

When cooked, serve the pudding piping hot, straight from the basin. This was traditionally served with parsley sauce.

Maidstone is the county town of Kent. In the 17th and 18th centuries Maidstone's position as chief market town for the region brought it great prosperity, due to the rich farmland, orchards and hop gardens that surrounded it. The easy transport of the River Medway, 'the highway of Kent', could supply local produce to the great London market with ease.

MAIDSTONE, MARKET PLACE 1885 12684a

ALLINGTON, THE CASTLE c1965 A230023

On the outskirts of Maidstone is Allington Castle, the ancestral home of the prominent Wyatt (Wiat) family in the past. A 15th-century member of the family is commemorated in an interesting memorial in the Church of St Mary the Virgin and All Saints at Boxley, north east of Maidstone. Sir Henry Wyatt was imprisoned in the Tower of London in 1483 for denying Richard III's right to the crown. The stone memorial above the choirstalls of the church reads: 'To the memory of Sir Henry Wiat, of Alington Casle, Knight banneret, descended of that ancient family, who was imprisoned and tortured in the Tower, in the reign of King Richard the third, kept in the dungeon, where [he was] fed and preserved by a cat…'. Sir Henry had been left cold and starving in his cell in the Tower, but he befriended a cat that found its way in and kept him company. The cat kept him warm by sleeping on his chest at night and brought him pigeons that it had caught, which the warder agreed to cook for him to eat, thus saving his life.

KENTISH PIGEONS IN A POT WITH PLUMS

There are a number of recipes from Kent which combine fruit with meat or game, such as lamb with cherries. This old recipe recalls the pigeons that saved Sir Henry Wiat's life in the Tower of London in 1483 (see opposite). The combination of fruit and game works very well, with the slightly sharp flavour of plums cutting through the richness of the meat. This amount serves four, allowing one pigeon per person.

> 4 young pigeons, prepared for cooking
> 25g/1oz butter
> 1 tablespoonful vegetable oil
> 2 teaspoonfuls plain flour
> Salt and freshly ground black pepper
> 1 onion, peeled and finely chopped
> 2 cloves
> 1 tablespoonful of chopped fresh mixed herbs, such as rosemary,
>   sage, parsley and thyme (or 1 teaspoonful of dried mixed herbs)
> 100ml/4 fl oz port
> 450g/1 lb fresh purple plums, stoned and cut into halves
> A pinch of freshly grated nutmeg

Pre-heat the oven to 170°C/325°F/Gas Mark 3. Put the flour in a bowl and season it with salt and pepper. Roll the pigeons in the flour so that they are lightly coated, and shake off any excess. Heat the butter and oil together in a large frying pan, then add the pigeons to the pan and fry them for a few minutes, turning them several times until they are lightly browned all over. Lift out the pigeons and put them into a large ovenproof casserole. Put the chopped onion in the pan and fry gently in the remaining fat until it is it soft and transparent. Spoon the cooked onion over the pigeons, then sprinkle the herbs over the top and add the cloves to the casserole. Pour the port into the frying pan and bring it to the boil, then pour it over the pigeons. Arrange the halved plums over the top. Cover the dish with a tight-fitting lid, and bake in the centre of the pre-heated oven for about 1½ hours, until the pigeons are tender. When ready to serve, transfer the pigeons and the plums to warmed serving plates, and keep warm. Boil up the remaining juices in the dish for 3-5 minutes to reduce down and make a sauce. Season the sauce to taste with salt, pepper and a little nutmeg, then pour it over the pigeons and serve immediately.

KENTISH CHEESES

It used to be said that the south-east of England has no tradition of cheese-making, but that has changed in recent years and there are now a number of dairy, sheep and goat farms producing milk, yogurt and cheeses, as well as some wonderful artisan cheesemakers. The list of cheesemakers in the county is growing all the time, but here are a few Kentish cheeses to look out for:

One of the local cheeses that Kent now offers is Kentish Blue, an unpasteurised mould-ripened blue cheese made by Kingcott Cheese Ltd at Iden Manor Farm near Staplehurst with milk from their own herd of dairy cows. Kentish Blue can be used in cooking in the same way as the better-known Stilton or Shropshire Blue cheeses from elsewhere in England.

The Kent Cheese Company of Penstock Hall Farm, based on the Wye Downs at East Brabourne, near Ashford, also make cheese using milk from their own dairy herd. Their range includes the crumbly, tangy Kentish Crown, Chaucer's Choice, a rich, flavourful soft-ripened cheese, Penstock Blue and Brabourne Brie.

Also making fine Kentish cheeses are the Winterdale Cheesemakers at Platt House Farm, Wrotham, near Sevenoaks. This company uses the milk from its farm to make a Kentish Camembert as well as Winterdale Shaw, a hard cheese which is cloth-bound and then matured in a stone cellar dug into the chalk of the North Downs, a process that produces a cheese that is full of flavour.

Syndale Valley Cheese of Faversham are makers of fresh soft cheeses flavoured with garlic, chives or peppercorns, Grove End Farmhouse, Tunstall Truckle and a range of goat's milk cheeses.

RECIPE

KENTISH RAREBIT

There are many different versions of 'rarebit' around Britain, but they all comprise of melted cheese on toast in some form. Here is the Kentish version, which includes apples. This makes 6 helpings of rarebit, so increase the quantities if you need to make more.

> 3 dessert apples, peeled, cored and sliced
> 50g/2oz butter or margarine
> 350g/12oz Cheddar cheese, grated
> Freshly ground black pepper to taste
> 6 slices of bread

Melt the butter or margarine in a large saucepan. Cook the apple slices very gently in the melted butter until they are soft, being careful not to let them brown. When the apples are cooked, add the grated cheese and pepper to taste, and mix it all well together.

Toast the bread slices and heat the grill to hot. Spread the apple and cheese mixture on the toasted bread, then place the slices under the hot grill and cook until the mixture is browned and bubbling.

RECIPE

BROCCOLI AND BLUE CHEESE FLAN

Kent's warm, moist climate and rich soil makes the county exceptionally fertile. Fruit and vegetables have been grown in abundance since the 16th century, and a particularly important crop is broccoli – Kent is one of the main broccoli-producing areas of the UK. If possible, use a Kent-made cheese such as Kentish Blue or Penstock Blue cheese to make this savoury flan, but otherwise any other hard blue cheese can be used, such as Stilton or Shropshire Blue. This can be served either warm or cold for summer lunches with a salad, or taken on a picnic to eat cold.

> 225g/8oz trimmed weight of broccoli florets
> 175g/6oz plain flour
> 75g/3oz butter or margarine
> Salt and freshly ground black pepper
> 175g/6oz blue cheese of choice (see above),
>   rinded and cut into thin slices
> 3 eggs, beaten
> 300ml/ ½ pint fresh milk, or single cream
> 1 medium onion, peeled and finely chopped
> 1 tablespoonful finely snipped fresh chives (optional)

Pre-heat the oven to 200°F/400°F/Gas Mark 6. Grease a flan dish about 25cms (10 inches) square or diameter, or a quiche tin with a removable base if you have one. Put the flour into a mixing bowl with a pinch of salt, and rub the butter or margarine into the flour until the mixture resembles fine breadcrumbs. Add 2-3 tablespoonfuls of cold water, just enough to mix it together to form a firm dough, then knead the dough lightly until it is smooth and elastic. Roll out the pastry dough on a floured surface, and use it to line the flan tin. Place a piece of greaseproof paper with some baking beans on the pastry base, and bake it blind for 10 minutes, until the pastry is set but not too browned, then remove the beans and paper and cook for a further 5 minutes to dry out the base. Remove from the oven, and reduce the oven temperature to 190°C/375°F/Gas Mark 5.

IGHTHAM, THE SQUARE 1901 47623

While the pastry case is cooking, prepare the broccoli florets. Bring a pan of water to the boil, and add the trimmed florets. Bring the water back to the boil, cook for 2 minutes, then remove from the heat and drain the broccoli thoroughly. Place the slices of cheese (and any crumbs) over the pastry base, then arrange the broccoli florets in the pastry case, on top of the cheese. Mix together the beaten eggs, the milk or cream, the chopped onion and chives (if using), and season to taste with freshly ground black pepper but only a little salt, if needed, as the cheese will already contain some salt. Pour the mixture into the pastry case. Bake in the oven at the reduced temperature for 40-45 minutes, until the flan is cooked but not dry, and the filling is risen and firm to the touch.

This should not be eaten hot straight from the oven, but leave it to cool a little and eat it warm, or otherwise eat it cold.

CHARTHAM, GIRLS IN A COUNTRY LANE
1906 53464x

RECIPE

CREAMED CABBAGE

Kent is also one of the main cabbage-producing areas of the UK. This recipe is an unusual and flavourful way of preparing cabbage, and is an ideal accompaniment to roast or grilled meat, and to sausages.

> 450g/1 lb cabbage
> 50g/2oz butter
> 1 clove of garlic, crushed or finely chopped
> Salt and freshly ground black pepper
> ¼ teaspoonful freshly grated nutmeg
> 90ml/3fl oz double cream.

Trim off any damaged leaves from the cabbage and discard. Quarter the cabbage, cut out and discard the hard core, then coarsely chop the rest of it.

Melt the butter in a heavy frying pan. Add the cabbage and the garlic. Fry gently, stirring frequently, for about 10 minutes, until the cabbage has softened a little but is still crunchy. Season to taste with salt, pepper and nutmeg, and stir in the cream. Cook for a further 5 minutes, stirring frequently, then remove from the heat and serve at once.

MARGATE, DONKEYS ON THE SANDS 1906 54759

The area of Kent known as the Isle of Thanet was indeed an offshore island in the past, but it is now joined to the rest of Kent across an expanse of fertile farmland reclaimed from the sea. The Isle of Thanet is famous not only as Kent's leisure coast, but also as an important area of vegetable production, particularly for the cultivation of fine-quality cauliflowers. Thanet has its own microclimate that is ideal for growing this vegetable, and for many years the acres of cauliflower fields around Broadstairs, Margate and Ramsgate were a feature of the landscape. Thanet's cauliflower production has declined in recent years, partly due to the poor returns the growers have received from supermarkets and partly because this vegetable seems to be going out of fashion, so much so that in recent years the Brassica Growers' Association (BGA) instigated a 'Save the Cauliflower' campaign.

RECIPE

CAULIFLOWER SOUFFLÉS

Most people just associate the cauliflower with Cauliflower Cheese, but here is something a bit different to celebrate the proud place of the cauliflower in Kent's food and farming heritage. This dish will not wait before serving, so make sure that people are ready to eat it as soon as it is cooked. This quantity serves 4.

    115/4oz small cauliflower florets (prepared weight)
    Salt and pepper
    25g/1oz butter, and extra butter for preparing the ramekin dishes
    1½ tablespoonfuls of plain flour
    100ml/4fl oz milk
    1 dessertspoonful wholegrain mustard
    50g/2oz mature tasty Cheddar, grated
    2 eggs, separated

Pre-heat the oven to 180°C/350°F/Gas Mark 4. Butter four individual ramekin dishes. Bring a saucepan of salted water to the boil and add the cauliflower florets. Cover the pan and simmer rapidly for about 10 minutes, until the florets are tender, then drain. Now make a white sauce. Melt the butter in a saucepan then stir in the flour. Gradually stir in the milk, a little at a time, then bring to the boil, stirring continually, until the mixture boils and is thick and smooth. Reduce the heat and simmer for 2 minutes. Stir in the mustard, and season to taste. Leave to cool a little, then put the sauce and the cooked cauliflower florets through a blender or liquidizer to make a thick purée, then turn it into a bowl and leave to cool for a few minutes. Stir in the grated cheese and the beaten egg yolks and mix well. Whisk the egg whites until they are stiff, then use a large metal spoon to fold them into the sauce mixture. Spoon the mixture into the prepared ramekins, and bake in the pre-heated oven for about 25 minutes, until they are risen and firm to the touch. Serve immediately.

TUNBRIDGE WELLS, THE PANTILES c1890 T87001

RECIPE

PARSNIP FLAN

Puddings, pies and tarts made with sweet root vegetables such as carrots, pumpkins and parsnips often appeared in recipe books of the 18th and 19th centuries. This old recipe from Kent uses parsnips to make a sweet flan with a creamy filling like lemon curd. It was traditional to decorate it with sugared primrose flowers when served in springtime.

> 175g/6oz plain flour
> 115g/4oz butter or margarine
> Pinch of salt
> 700g/1½ lbs parsnips
> 2 tablespoonfuls thick honey
> 1 level teaspoonful ground ginger
> ½ teaspoonful ground mixed spice
> ¼ teaspoonful freshly grated nutmeg
> 2 egg yolks
> Juice and grated rind of 2 lemons

Pre-heat the oven to 200°C/400°F/Gas Mark 6. Grease a 20-24cm (8-9 inch) flan dish or pie tin. First, make the pastry. Put the flour and salt in a bowl and rub in the butter or margarine. Mix in just enough cold water to bind the mixture together. Gather the dough into a ball and lightly knead it until it is smooth and elastic. Cover the dough with cling film and put it in the fridge to 'rest' until needed. Peel and quarter the parsnips, and remove the woody centre from any older parsnips. Cook the parsnips in boiling water until they are soft – the time will depend on the age of the parsnips you are using. When cooked and tender, drain them well and mash them thoroughly to a soft pulp. Add the honey, spices, egg yolks and grated lemon rind and juice, and mix it all together thoroughly. Roll out the pastry dough on a lightly floured surface, and use it to line the flan tin or plate. Trim the edges, reserving the trimmings. Spoon the parsnip mixture into the pastry case. Roll out the pastry trimmings and cut them into thin strips, then make a lattice pattern with them across the top of the flan, twisting them to look pretty. Crimp all round the flan by pressing down with the end of a fork and your thumb so that you get a pattern around the pastry edge, and the strips are firmly stuck down. Bake in the pre-heated oven for 30-35 minutes until the pastry is golden-brown.

RECIPE

CANTERBURY PUDDING

75g/3oz self-raising flour
75g/3oz fresh breadcrumbs
75g/3oz shredded suet
50g/2oz caster sugar
1 lemon, grated zest and juice
1 egg, beaten
3 tablespoonfuls brandy
3 tablespoonfuls milk

Pre-heat the oven to 180°C/350°F/Gas Mark 4.
Grease a 1.1 litre (2 pint) pudding dish.

Mix together the flour, breadcrumbs, suet and sugar,
and stir in the lemon zest. Make a well in the centre
and mix in the beaten egg, lemon juice, brandy and
enough milk to give a soft dropping consistency.

Pour the mixture into the greased pudding dish and
bake in the pre-heated oven, uncovered, for about 1
hour until the pudding is well risen. Serve hot, with
custard or cream.

CANTERBURY, WEST GATE c1880 C18301

This photograph (above) shows the massive twin-towered West Gate in Canterbury, the only survivor of the medieval gates that once interrupted the path of the wall around the city. Canterbury was the scene of disturbances known as 'The Plum Pudding Riots' in 1647. The riots took place during the Civil War after Christmas celebrations in Canterbury were banned by Puritan extremists. The streets of the city were filled with Royalist rioters, and people declared they were on the side of 'God, King Charles and Kent'. In retaliation, Oliver Cromwell ordered the sector of Canterbury's city walls between the castle and the West Gate to be demolished.

35

RECIPE

KENTISH PUDDING PIE

This is a very old recipe from Kent which is rather like a baked cheesecake, and can be eaten hot or cold. It was particularly popular around Folkestone, and is also known as Folkestone Pudding Pie. It was called a pudding pie because of the way it is made – partly boiled, like a pudding, and partly baked in the oven, like a pie. It is also known as Lenten Pie, as it was traditionally eaten during Lent, the period leading up to Easter.

225g/8oz shortcrust pastry
600ml/1 pint of milk
50g/2oz ground rice
50g/2oz butter
25g/1oz caster sugar
2 eggs, beaten
50g/2oz currants
¼ teaspoonful mixed spice
Finely grated rind of 1 lemon
2 tablespoonfuls of double cream
¼ teaspoonful freshly grated nutmeg

Pre-heat the oven to 200°F/400°F/Gas Mark 6. Line a greased pie or flan dish with the pastry. Place a piece of greaseproof paper with some baking beans on the pastry base, and bake it blind for 10 minutes, then remove the beans and paper and cook for a further 5 minutes to dry out the base. Reduce the oven temperature to 180°C/350°F/Gas Mark 4, and place a baking tray in the oven to heat up.

Put the ground rice into a basin and mix it to a smooth cream with 2 tablespoonfuls of the milk, then put the rest of the milk and the sugar into a saucepan and bring to the boil. Pour the boiling milk onto the ground rice, stirring all the time, then put the mixture back into the saucepan and bring back to the boil, then reduce the heat and simmer for 5 minutes, stirring occasionally, as the mixture thickens and cooks. Remove the pan from the heat and allow the mixture to cool. Cream the butter with the sugar until it is light and fluffy, then gradually beat in the eggs, a little at a time, taking care that the mixture does not curdle. Add the cooled ground rice mixture, the currants, mixed spice and lemon rind, and beat well. Stir in the cream, then pour the mixture into the pie or flan dish. Sprinkle the top with some freshly grated nutmeg. Stand the dish on the baking sheet in the centre of the pre-heated oven (this helps the pastry base to cook properly) and bake for 35-40 minutes, until the top is risen and golden and the filling is firm.

RECIPE

KENTISH WELL PUDDING

The addition of currants to this recipe is what makes it a Kentish Well Pudding – another version, which omits the currants but has a whole lemon inside, is known as Sussex Pond Pudding. Both recipes originate from the Kentish/Sussex Weald, where there was an important iron industry between the 16th to 18th centuries. The butter and brown sugar inside the pudding cooks to a delicious sweet sauce which spills out around the serving dish like a pond when the pudding is cut open, reminiscent of the hammer ponds of the Wealden iron industry.

> 225g/8oz self-raising flour
> 115g/4oz shredded suet
> A pinch of salt
> 50g/2oz currants, raisins or sultanas
> 115g/4oz butter, cut into small pieces
> 115g/4oz soft brown or demerara sugar
> Grated rind of 1 lemon

Sift the flour into a bowl and stir in the suet and salt. Mix in just enough water to form it into a fairly soft but workable dough. Roll out two thirds of the dough on a lightly floured surface to form a large round and use it to line a well-buttered 1.2 litre (2 pint) pudding basin. Press most of the dried fruit evenly into the dough, to give the pudding a fruity lining, reserving a dessertspoonful.

Cut the butter into small pieces and put half the sugar and half the butter pieces into the pudding, together with half the lemon rind. Roll out a small, thin piece of pastry dough and lay it across the filling, then put the rest of the currants, butter pieces, sugar and lemon rind on top of it. Roll out the remaining pastry to make a round lid for

the pudding, dampen the edge of the crust at the top of the basin and place the lid on the pudding, sealing the edges well by pressing them together. Cover the pudding basin with its lid, if you have one, otherwise cover it closely with a lid made from a pleated piece of greaseproof paper (to allow room for the pudding to expand and rise during cooking), followed by a piece of pleated foil, firmly tied on with string. Place the basin in a large saucepan of boiling water, cover the pan with its lid, and steam over boiling water for 2½ -3 hours. Top up the pan with more boiling water from time to time, and be sure not to let the pan boil dry.

When the pudding is cooked, lift the basin from the pan and 'rest' the pudding for a few minutes before serving. Then remove the foil and invert the pudding onto a deep, wide serving dish – make sure the dish is big enough to catch the sauce as the pudding is cut open. If preferred, the pudding can be 'finished off' in a low oven for a few minutes, to dry off. Serve with custard or cream.

RECIPE

PLUM AND WALNUT CRUMBLE

Historically known as 'The Garden of England', Kent grows much of the country's home-produced fruit, especially apples, pears, cherries and plums, particularly Victoria plums. This recipe uses the plums that the county is famous for in a rich crumble that also includes walnuts. Although Kent is famous for its cob nuts (a variety of large hazelnut - see page 52), some farmers in Kent are now starting to cultivate walnuts commercially as a result of changing climate conditions, which is making their crop more reliable.

> 75g/3oz walnut pieces
> 75g/3oz butter or margarine, diced
> 175g/6oz plain flour
> 175g/6oz demerara sugar
> 1kg/2 lbs plums, halved and stoned

Pre-heat the oven to 180°C/350°F/Gas Mark 4, and butter a large ovenproof dish.

Spread the nuts on a baking sheet and place in the oven for 8-10 minutes, until they are evenly coloured.

Put the plums into the dish and stir in the toasted nuts and half the demerara sugar. Rub the butter or margarine into the flour until the mixture resembles coarse crumbs. Stir in the remaining sugar and continue to rub in until fine crumbs are formed. Cover the fruit with the crumb mixture and press it down lightly. Bake the pudding in the pre-heated oven for about 45 minutes, until the top is golden brown and the fruit tender. Serve with custard or cream.

RECIPE

KENTISH CHERRY BATTER PUDDING

Cherries are believed to have been introduced into Britain by the Romans and have always thrived in Kent. Sadly, cherry production in the county has declined in recent years because harvesting the fruit is such a labour-intensive business, but 90% of English cherries are still grown in Kent. The most common dessert varieties are Stella and Sunburst, whilst Morello cherries are mainly used for cooking. Many of the old traditional cherry dishes from Kent still survive, the most famous of which is probably Cherry Batter Pudding.

> 3 tablespoonfuls of kirsch (a cherry brandy – optional)
> 450g/1 lb dark cherries, pitted
> 50g/2oz plain flour
> 50g/2oz caster sugar
> 2 eggs, separated
> 300ml/ ½ pint milk
> 75g/3oz butter, melted

Sprinkle the kirsch, if used, over the cherries in a small bowl, and leave them to soak for about 30 minutes. Mix the flour and sugar together, then slowly stir in the egg yolks and milk to make a smooth batter. Stir in half the melted butter, and leave for 30 minutes.

Pre-heat the oven to 220°C/425°F/Gas Mark 7. Pour the remaining butter into a 600ml (1 pint) ovenproof dish, and put the dish in the oven to heat. Whisk the egg whites until stiff, then fold them into the batter with the cherries and kirsch, if used, and pour the mixture into the baking dish. Bake for about 15 minutes, then reduce the oven temperature to 180°C/350°F/Gas Mark 4 and bake for a further 20 minutes, until golden and set in the centre. Serve hot, sprinkled with sugar, with custard or cream.

RECIPE

CRANBROOK CHERRY AND ALMOND FLAN

This delicious recipe from Cranbrook encases cherries in a buttery, almond filling. The amounts given here will make a flan large enough for 2-3 people, so increase the quantities to feed more.

> 450g/1 lb cherries, de-stoned or not, as you prefer
> A few drops of almond essence
> 1 medium-sized egg (it should weigh as close as possible to 50g/2oz – if you are using a larger egg, the other ingredients listed below should be the same weight as the egg)
> 50g/2oz self-raising flour
> 50g/2oz butter, softened to room temperature
> 50g/2oz caster sugar
> 50g/2oz ground almonds

Pre-heat the oven to 180°C/350°F/Gas Mark 4.

Grease a shallow ovenproof dish and arrange the cherries in it. Cream the butter and the sugar together in a bowl until the mixture is light and fluffy. Gradually beat in the egg, a little at a time so that the mixture does not curdle, then use a large metal spoon to fold in the flour, the ground almonds and the almond essence.

Spread the mixture evenly over the cherries in the dish, then bake in the pre-heated oven for 20-25 minutes, until the mixture is risen and golden brown, and firm to the touch. Serve with custard or cream.

CRANBROOK, STONE STREET 1906 56971

RECIPE

GYPSY TART

This tart originated in Kent, where many people remember it as a favourite feature of school dinners. It is very easy to make, and the dark muscovado sugar gives the sweet filling a delicious flavour. Its name is reminiscent of the many Gypsies who used to come to Kent in the summer and autumn to help with the fruit and hop picking. If you don't want to make the pastry yourself, use a ready-made pastry case.

> For the pastry:
> 225g/8oz plain flour
> A pinch of salt
> 140g/5oz butter or margarine
> 1 egg, beaten
> For the filling:
> 1 x 410g (14oz) tin of evaporated milk,
>   chilled in the fridge overnight
> 275g/10oz soft dark brown (muscovado) sugar

Pre-heat the oven to 200°C/400°C/Gas Mark 6. Grease a flan dish or tin, about 25cm (10 inches) in diameter. Put the flour into a mixing bowl with the salt, and rub in the butter or margarine. Add 2-3 tablespoonfuls of cold water, just enough to form a firm dough, then knead the dough lightly until it is smooth. Roll out the dough on a floured surface, and use it to line the flan dish. Place a piece of greaseproof paper with some baking beans on the pastry base, and bake it blind for 10 minutes, then remove the beans and paper and cook for a further 5 minutes to dry out the base. Remove from the oven, take out the beans and paper and leave the pastry base to cool.

Using an electric whisk or mixer, whisk together the chilled evaporated milk and sugar on full power until the mixture has become light, fluffy, and coffee-coloured – this will take some time, about 12-15 minutes. The consistency should be like softly whipped cream, but not holding peaks. Pour the mixture into the cooled pastry case and bake in the pre-heated oven for 10 minutes, when the filling will have developed a sticky surface. Remove from the oven and leave the tart to cool completely, by which time the filling will be set and the tart will be ready to serve.

GOUDHURST, HOP PICKERS 1904 52569

A major part of Kent's economy in the past was the growing of hops, used for flavouring and preserving beer. The hop production that was once widespread in Kent is commemorated by the Whitbread Hop Farm at Paddock Wood, now a popular museum. Hops are ready for picking in early September. Harvesting the hops is now done by machines, but for many years the hop cones were picked by hand. This was a very labour intensive affair, and at hop picking time great numbers of seasonal labourers would descend on the hop gardens; these hop pickers were made up of local people, Gypsies, and whole families from the East End of London who treated hop picking as an annual working holiday. Some farms had hop pickers' huts in the hop gardens for their use, and often the families would bring their own wallpaper to make the place homely during their stay.

RECIPE

KENTISH HOP-PICKERS CAKE

This moist, spicy cake was made by farmers' wives to serve at teatime to hungry pickers in Kent's hop gardens at the time of the hop harvest. This recipe can be made as two smaller cakes if preferred, baked in two 450g/1 lb loaf tins.

> 275g/10oz self-raising flour
> 1 teaspoonful ground ginger
> 1 teaspoonful mixed spice
> 175g/6oz butter or margarine,
>   softened to room temperature
> 115g/4oz soft brown sugar
> 115g/4oz sultanas
> 115g/4oz currants
> 50g/2oz mixed peel
> 425ml/ ¾ pint milk
> 1 tablespoonful black treacle
> 1 level teaspoonful cream of tartar
> Half a level teaspoonful bicarbonate of soda

Pre-heat the oven to 160°C/325°F/Gas Mark 3. Grease and line a 900g/2 lb loaf tin.

Sift the flour and spices into a bowl and rub in the butter or margarine. Mix in the sugar and dried fruit. Warm the milk in a small pan with the treacle, add the cream of tartar and bicarbonate of soda and stir together until dissolved. Gradually add the liquid into the dry ingredients, and beat the mixture together well – it should be of a consistency to drop from the mixing spoon. Turn the mixture into the prepared tin. Bake in the middle of the pre-heated oven for about 1½ hours, until the cake is firm to the touch and a skewer inserted into it comes out clean. Leave the cake to cool in the tin before turning out onto a wire rack. Store in an airtight tin – this cake keeps well.

RECIPE

OAST CAKES

These small fried cakes are named after the oast houses in which hops were taken to be dried after being picked. The oast houses were basically kilns, or ovens, where the piles of hops were dried on sacking laid over wooden slats, and heated by fires of anthracite mixed with sulphur. The fumes escaped through the distinctively shaped cowls at the top. The hop-drying process has now been modernised, and many old oast houses are now used as storerooms or have been converted into unusual and distinctively shaped houses. Oast cakes were a favourite with the hop-pickers, who would mix the dough in the morning, then form it into small balls and fry them over a camp fire for the afternoon break. Oast cakes were also traditionally eaten at a Kentish hop feast, which was known as a 'hopkin'. A small amount of lemon juice is mixed with the water in this recipe, but the water is mixed with parsnip wine or even beer in some old recipes.

> 225g/8oz plain flour
> Half a teaspoonful baking powder
> Half a teaspoonful of salt
> 50g/2oz lard, butter or margarine, cut into small pieces
> 50g/2oz caster sugar
> 75g/3oz currants
> 3-4 tablespoonfuls of water, mixed with one teaspoonful
> of lemon juice
> Oil, for frying

Sift the flour, baking powder and salt together into a mixing bowl. Rub in the lard, butter or margarine until the mixture resembles fine breadcrumbs. Add the sugar and currants, then mix with enough of the water and lemon juice to form a soft dough. Roll out the dough and cut it into 5cm (2 inch) rounds. Heat the oil in a heavy-based frying pan and fry the oast cakes, a few at a time, for 2-3 minutes on each side, until they are golden brown. Drain on kitchen paper, dredge with caster sugar, and eat whilst they are still hot.

ASHFORD, WOMEN CYCLISTS, CANTERBURY ROAD 1908 60331x

The River Medway divides Kent into two halves with regard to the terms used for the county's male inhabitants. If they live to the east and south of the Medway they are 'Men of Kent', whilst to the north and west they are 'Kentishmen'. However, women all over the county are 'Maids of Kent', a reference to Joan, the 'Fair Maid of Kent' (1328-85), the daughter of Edmund of Woodstock, 1st Earl of Kent, who was known for her great beauty. She married Edward the Black Prince, the eldest son of Edward III, and was the first English Princess of Wales. Amongst the dishes made by Kentish Maids over the centuries were Kentish huffkins. These are small flat loaves with a soft crust, which are made with a dimple in the middle. They can either be eaten sliced and buttered as a teabread, or as a dessert, with their indentation filled with soft fruit – a traditional Kentish dessert is a huffkin filled with hot cherries. You won't find huffkins in many shops nowadays, but they are easy to make yourself, and a recipe is given on the opposite page.

RECIPE

KENTISH HUFFKINS

This amount should make 10 huffkins.

> 450g/1 lb plain white flour
> Half a teaspoonful salt
> 25g/1oz lard or margarine
> 1½ teaspoonfuls dried yeast
> 1 teaspoonful caster sugar
> 300ml/ ½ pint milk and water mixed, warmed

Sprinkle the dried yeast into the warmed milk and water, together with the sugar. Leave in a warm place for about 15 minutes, for the yeast to activate and mixture to go frothy.

Sift the flour and salt into a bowl and rub in the lard or margarine. Make a well in the centre and pour in the milk and yeast mixture, and mix it all together to form a soft dough that leaves the sides of the bowl clean. Turn out the dough onto a floured surface and knead for about 10 minutes, until the dough is smooth and elastic. Place the dough in a clean bowl and cover the bowl with a tea-towel, or place it inside a plastic bag, and leave in a warm place for one hour, until the dough has doubled in size. Turn out the dough again on to a floured surface and knead lightly for a minute or so, then divide the dough into 10 flat oval cakes about 1cm (½ inch) thick. Grease two baking trays. Place the cakes on the trays, leaving room between them for expansion, cover and leave again in a warm place for a further 30 minutes, until they are well risen and have doubled in size.

Pre-heat the oven to 225°C/425°F/Gas Mark 7. When the huffkins are well risen, use your floured thumb to indent a hollow in the centre of each one. Bake the huffkins for 15-20 minutes until they are lightly browned and firm. Remove from the oven and cover them immediately with a clean, dry cloth until they are completely cold; this helps to keep them soft.

RECIPE

LATTICE APPLE CAKE

Apple growing is big business in Kent, and the county has long been famous for the apples grown there. As Charles Dickens wrote in 'The Pickwick Papers': 'Kent, sir - everybody knows Kent - apples, cherries, hops and women'. Kent is also the home of the UK National Fruit Collection, at Brogdale. Its 30 plus acres of orchards contain the largest collection of apple varieties in the world – more than 2,300 dessert, culinary and cider varieties can be found there. The Brogdale Farm orchards are open to the public, and special festivals are held there when you can taste the different varieties of apples, as well as other fruits in season, such as plums, pears, cherries and quinces.

> 200g/7oz self-raising flour
> A pinch of salt
> 150g/5oz butter or margarine, softened
> 75g/3oz caster sugar
> 1 egg, beaten
> 350g/12oz cooking apples
> Juice of half a lemon
> 2 tablespoonfuls of apricot jam
> 2 tablespoonfuls demerara sugar
> A little icing sugar, to finish (optional)

Pre-heat the oven to 160°C/325°F/Gas Mark 3. Grease and line a 20-24cm (8-9 inch) diameter cake tin. Cream together the butter and caster sugar until it is light and fluffy. Gradually beat in the egg, a little at a time, adding a little flour if necessary to prevent the mixture curding. Sieve the flour and salt into the bowl, and gently fold it into the mixture. Gently pat or roll out three-quarters of the mixture on a lightly floured surface, and fit it into the prepared tin. Peel and core the apples and cut them into slices. Sprinkle the apple slices with the lemon juice to prevent them discolouring. Arrange the slices in an overlapping pattern all over the cake mixture.

Warm the jam, then brush it all over the apples, then sprinkle over the two tablespoonfuls of demerara sugar. Flour your hands, then take small pieces of the remaining cake mixture and roll them out with your hands into strips, and arrange them across the top of the cake in a lattice pattern over the apples.

Bake the cake above the middle of the pre-heated oven for one hour. Leave the cake in the tin for 5 minutes, then turn out on a wire rack and leave to cool. Dust with a little icing sugar before serving if you wish.

TENTERDEN, HIGH STREET 1900 44994

RECIPE

COBNUT BISCUITS

Kent is famous for its cobnuts and filberts, cultivated varieties of hazelnut that are full of flavour and have a pleasant, sweet taste. However, the famous Kent Cob is not, in fact, a round cobnut, but actually a filbert, which is more elongated in form. It is one of the best forms of hazelnut. Kent Cobs, originally and more correctly called Lambert's Filberts, were first grown by a Mr Lambert in the 1800s. Use Kentish cobnuts in this recipe if you can find them, but otherwise any hazelnuts you can buy will be fine. This quantity makes about 16 biscuits.

> 115g/4oz shelled whole cobnuts or hazelnuts
> (or use ready-chopped nuts, and omit the roasting stage in the recipe)
> 150g/5oz plain flour
> A pinch of salt
> 115g/4oz butter, softened
> 50g/2oz caster sugar

If using whole nuts, spread them in a roasting tray and toast them in a moderate oven (190°C/375°F/Gas Mark 5) for 10 minutes, then rub off their skins. Grind the nuts to a powder in a coffee mill or blender (this is easier to do if you roughly chop the whole nuts first). Don't worry if there are a few bits of nut left in your 'nut flour' – this will add interest to the biscuits. Cream together the butter and sugar, then add the flour, salt and ground nuts and mix it all together well. Knead the dough for a few minutes, then chill it in the fridge for 30 minutes. Pre-heat the oven to 190°C/375°F/Gas Mark 5. Grease a baking tray and line it with greaseproof paper. Roll out the dough to about 1cm (half an inch) thick, and cut it into rounds about 5cm (2 inches) in diameter with a biscuit cutter. Place the biscuits on the prepared baking tray and bake in the pre-heated oven for 7-10 minutes, until they are golden but not too browned – it is important not to overcook them. Remove from the oven and leave to cool on the tray for five minutes to firm up slightly, then put them a wire tray to cool completely. Store in an airtight container.

In medieval times the village of Biddenden, north of Tenterden, was the home of the Biddenden Maids, Eliza and Mary Chulkhurst, who feature on the village sign. The Maids were Siamese twins who were born joined together at the hips and shoulders, and lived like that for 34 years. When one Maid died, the other refused to be separated, and she died a few hours later. After their deaths, the sisters bequeathed 20 acres of land in trust for the village, the income to be spent on the sick and needy and also to provide a gift of bread and cheese for the poor on Easter Monday morning, known as the Biddenden Dole. This is still given out in Biddenden each year, although the bread and cheese now takes the form of a commemorative biscuit known as a Biddenden Cake, which bears a picture of the two sisters.

**BIDDENDEN
THE VILLAGE SIGN
c1955** B88014a

FRANCIS FRITH

PIONEER VICTORIAN PHOTOGRAPHER

Francis Frith, founder of the world-famous photographic archive, was a complex and multi-talented man. A devout Quaker and a highly successful Victorian businessman, he was philosophical by nature and pioneering in outlook. By 1855 he had already established a wholesale grocery business in Liverpool, and sold it for the astonishing sum of £200,000, which is the equivalent today of over £15,000,000. Now in his thirties, and captivated by the new science of photography, Frith set out on a series of pioneering journeys up the Nile and to the Near East.

INTRIGUE AND EXPLORATION

He was the first photographer to venture beyond the sixth cataract of the Nile. Africa was still the mysterious 'Dark Continent', and Stanley and Livingstone's historic meeting was a decade into the future. The conditions for picture taking confound belief. He laboured for hours in his wicker dark-room in the sweltering heat of the desert, while the volatile chemicals fizzed dangerously in their trays. Back in London he exhibited his photographs and was 'rapturously cheered' by members of the Royal Society. His reputation as a photographer was made overnight.

VENTURE OF A LIFE-TIME

By the 1870s the railways had threaded their way across the country, and Bank Holidays and half-day Saturdays had been made obligatory by Act of Parliament. All of a sudden the working man and his family were able to enjoy days out, take holidays, and see a little more of the world.

With typical business acumen, Francis Frith foresaw that these new tourists would enjoy having souvenirs to commemorate their days out. For the next thirty years he travelled the country by train and by pony and trap, producing fine photographs of seaside resorts and beauty spots that were keenly bought by millions of Victorians. These prints were painstakingly pasted into family albums and pored over during the dark nights of winter, rekindling precious memories of summer excursions. Frith's studio was soon supplying retail shops all over the country, and by 1890 F Frith & Co had become the greatest specialist photographic publishing company in the world, with over 2,000 sales outlets, and pioneered the picture postcard.

FRANCIS FRITH'S LEGACY

Francis Frith had died in 1898 at his villa in Cannes, his great project still growing. By 1970 the archive he created contained over a third of a million pictures showing 7,000 British towns and villages.

Frith's legacy to us today is of immense significance and value, for the magnificent archive of evocative photographs he created provides a unique record of change in the cities, towns and villages throughout Britain over a century and more. Frith and his fellow studio photographers revisited locations many times down the years to update their views, compiling for us an enthralling and colourful pageant of British life and character.

We are fortunate that Frith was dedicated to recording the minutiae of everyday life. For it is this sheer wealth of visual data, the painstaking chronicle of changes in dress, transport, street layouts, buildings, housing and landscape that captivates us so much today, offering us a powerful link with the past and with the lives of our ancestors.

Computers have now made it possible for Frith's many thousands of images to be accessed almost instantly. The archive offers every one of us an opportunity to examine the places where we and our families have lived and worked down the years. Its images, depicting our shared past, are now bringing pleasure and enlightenment to millions around the world a century and more after his death.

For further information visit: www.francisfrith.com

INTERIOR DECORATION

Frith's photographs can be seen framed and as giant wall murals in thousands of pubs, restaurants, hotels, banks, retail stores and other public buildings throughout Britain. These provide interesting and attractive décor, generating strong local interest and acting as a powerful reminder of gentler days in our increasingly busy and frenetic world.

FRITH PRODUCTS

All Frith photographs are available as prints and posters in a variety of different sizes and styles. In the UK we also offer a range of other gift and stationery products illustrated with Frith photographs, although many of these are not available for delivery outside the UK – see our web site for more information on the products available for delivery in your country.

THE INTERNET

Over 100,000 photographs of Britain can be viewed and purchased on the Frith web site. The web site also includes memories and reminiscences contributed by our customers, who have personal knowledge of localities and of the people and properties depicted in Frith photographs. If you wish to learn more about a specific town or village you may find these reminiscences fascinating to browse. Why not add your own comments if you think they would be of interest to others? See **www.francisfrith.com**

PLEASE HELP US BRING FRITH'S PHOTOGRAPHS TO LIFE

Our authors do their best to recount the history of the places they write about. They give insights into how particular towns and villages developed, they describe the architecture of streets and buildings, and they discuss the lives of famous people who lived there. But however knowledgeable our authors are, the story they tell is necessarily incomplete.

Frith's photographs are so much more than plain historical documents. They are living proofs of the flow of human life down the generations. They show real people at real moments in history; and each of those people is the son or daughter of someone, the brother or sister, aunt or uncle, grandfather or grandmother of someone else. All of them lived, worked and played in the streets depicted in Frith's photographs.

We would be grateful if you would give us your insights into the places shown in our photographs: the streets and buildings, the shops, businesses and industries. Post your memories of life in those streets on the Frith website: what it was like growing up there, who ran the local shop and what shopping was like years ago; if your workplace is shown tell us about your working day and what the building is used for now. Read other visitors' memories and reconnect with your shared local history and heritage. With your help more and more Frith photographs can be brought to life, and vital memories preserved for posterity, and for the benefit of historians in the future.

Wherever possible, we will try to include some of your comments in future editions of our books. Moreover, if you spot errors in dates, titles or other facts, please let us know, because our archive records are not always completely accurate—they rely on 140 years of human endeavour and hand-compiled records. You can email us using the contact form on the website.

Thank you!

For further information, trade, or author enquiries
please contact us at the address below:

**The Francis Frith Collection, Unit 6, Oakley Business Park,
Wylye Road, Dinton, Wiltshire SP3 5EU England.**
Tel: +44 (0)1722 716 376 Fax: +44 (0)1722 716 881
e-mail: sales@francisfrith.co.uk **www.francisfrith.com**